Contents

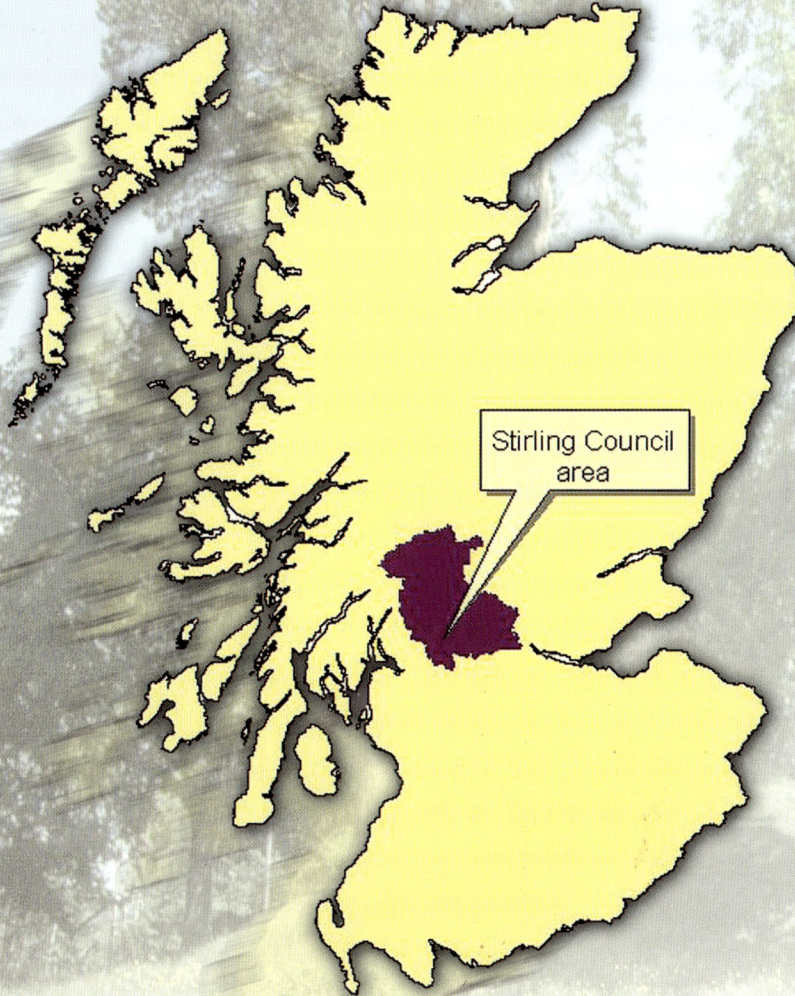

Stirling Council area

THE PEOPLE

Through the interpretation of the archaeological evidence this book tells of the first people who moved into the area around what became known as Stirling, and of the peoples who succeeded them, from prehistoric times up to the period of the Roman occupation. Stirling lies at a crossroads where influences from north and south, east and west meet. What happened here is part of a wider story, extending beyond current administrative boundaries. The book looks at relevant sites and objects which throw light on where and how the people of the area lived and died and their impact on their environment.

THE EVIDENCE

The Romans were the first to leave a written history in Britain and therefore our knowledge of prehistoric peoples relies heavily on archaeological evidence. Archaeology is the study of past societies primarily through their material remains - their buildings, tools and other artefacts as well as their personal physical remains. Archaeology is also concerned with how people organised themselves, how they exploited their environment, in their religious beliefs and how they communicated. A variety of techniques involving a range of scientific disciplines, such as palaeobotany, is available to assist archaeology in developing a fuller picture of the past. The use of two of these, aerial photography and radiocarbon dating, is explained on the next page.

Cropmarks

Cropmarks, identified through aerial photography, often indicate the existence of archaeological sites which are not otherwise visible on the ground. Much of today's agricultural land has been farmed for over 5000 years, but the traces of many monuments, which have been levelled over the years by ploughing, still survive today below the ground. The disturbance caused by an ancient ditch or pit can be identified from the air as cropmarks. Because they fill with soil which holds more moisture than undisturbed soils, such features allow the crops above them to grow taller, and to stay green while the crops around ripen.

In crops like wheat and barley, ditches appear from the air as dark green lines, while pits and postholes appear as dark patches. On the other hand, where features like walls or the hard surfaces of Roman roads survive, the crops above them receive less water, and dry out much more quickly. These show as lighter marks in the crop.

Killin

Tyndrum

Crianlarich

Lochearnhead

Strathyre

Brig o' Turk

Callander

Doune

Dunblane

Bridge of Allan

Aberfoyle

Thornhill

Buchlyvie

Kippen

Gargunnock

STIRLING

Fallin

Drymen

Balfron

Bannockburn

Cowie

Killearn

Fintry

Plean

Strathblane

Radiocarbon dating

Calibrated radiocarbon dates are used throughout this book. Radiocarbon dating was developed in the 1950's. For the first time, archaeologists had a means of dating organic remains - wood and charcoal, seeds and other plant remains and human or animal bone.

All plants and animals absorb carbon from the atmosphere in order to live and grow. When they die Carbon 14 (C14), the radioactive isotope naturally present in that carbon, decays at a known rate. By measuring the remaining proportion of C14 in any carbon sample discovered, it is possible to establish an approximate date of death.

The original assumption was that the concentration of C14 in the atmosphere has been constant through time. In the 1960s it was realised that it varied, largely due to fluctuations in the earth's magnetic field and this meant that radiocarbon dates were not the same as calendar dates. To provide real calendar dates the C14 dates needed to be adjusted by calibrating them against known dates - that is by comparing them to radiocarbon measurements on things with confirmed ages, like wood dated by counting tree-rings. Annual rings form under the bark of a tree during every growing season and the thickness of each ring is determined by the weather. The dating of tree rings, by linking the long-term patterns stored in them, is known as dendrochronology. Archaeological dating is at its most effective where the two methods can be used together.

ACCESS

Most of the archaeological sites described in this book are on private land and are not generally accessible to the public. The permission of the owner and tenant of the land should be sought by anyone wanting to visit them.

OBJECTS

Where known, the current location of the more important objects referred to in the book is given in the text. It should be noted that the items might not be on permanent display. At the time of writing some of the more important recent finds have not been allocated to a particular museum.

NEW ARRIVALS - THE HUNTER-GATHERERS
The Mesolithic 8000 - 4000 BC

Around 2 million years ago, due to major climatic deterioration, the onset of arctic conditions resulted in Scotland being covered with glaciers and ice sheets. Ice cover reached its maximum extent in the Stirling area between 17,000 and 20,000 years ago. During this last Ice Age there was a series of retreats and advances of the ice as temperatures fluctuated. Local sea level is known to have fallen at times well below that of the present day. The last glacier in the Forth Valley retreated towards Loch Lomond around 9-8000 BC. Sea level was then much higher than it is at present as the glacial meltwaters associated with this retreat returned to the sea. Around Doune, for example, the sea level has been shown to have been up to 49m above present levels. The relative height of the land then also rose as the weight of the ice disappeared. These fluctuations in relative land and sea levels are reflected in the survival of old shorelines and cliffs along the edge of the floodplain of the River Forth. Until the final melting of the ice, around 12,000 years ago, there is no evidence of human presence in Scotland.

The Environment and the First People

By 10,000 BC there was no longer permanent glacial ice in Scotland. The warmer climate which followed the gradual melting of the ice sheets allowed the renewed development of soils. Mixed woodlands of oak, hazel and elm eventually covered most of the lowlands, with mainly pine and birch in the highlands. Animals soon followed - bears, wolves, wild cattle, wild boar, red deer, and elk, as well as smaller animals such as beavers, along with fish, shellfish and birds.

During the eighth millennium BC, small bands of hunter-gatherers arrived in Scotland from the south. These first people are described as belonging to the Mesolithic or Middle Stone Age. They had no metal tools, pottery, domesticated plants or animals but they fashioned fine stone tools, often from flint. They lived a semi-nomadic way of life, taking advantage of the seasonal concentrations of game, such as geese and salmon, and the availability of nuts and berries. They hunted both large and small animals and birds, fished and gathered wild berries, fruits, nuts and fungi. It is likely that the bulk of the Mesolithic diet would have been produced by gathering rather than by hunting.

The hunting of larger game may have been a male activity while the hunting of smaller animals, gathering nuts and collecting plant foods would have been women's work. The women were probably also responsible for processing the carcasses. Wild animals, as well as providing meat and blood, were a source of skins, furs, sinews, and bone. Bone and antler were used for making tools.

An unusual barbed antler point found on the foreshore of the Forth near Blackness in 1993 is now in the collections of the National Museums of Scotland. As well as arrows, spears and harpoons, these hunter-fishers also made complex traps and nets for fish and other game.

Pollen analysis shows the impact of the Mesolithic people on their local environment. Pollen grains are fragile but they do survive in peat deposits and in lake sediments. By taking cores from these sediments and carbon dating them, palaeobotanists can provide information on changes in vegetation cover and therefore on the influences of both climate change and human interference.

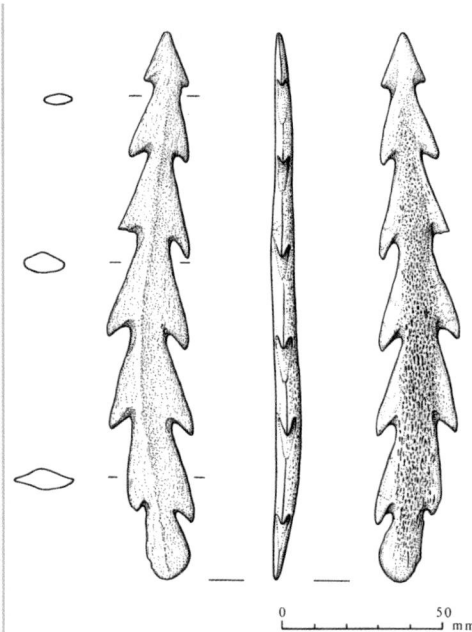

Barbed antler point from Blackness
Copyright Trustees of the National Museums of Scotland

This analysis confirms that the climate in the Mesolithic was warmer than today and that much more of the landscape was covered with trees and scrub providing shelter, food and raw materials. There is also evidence that clearings were created in the woods, perhaps through burning, to help the hunters by providing better grazing areas for wild animals or to encourage the growth of particular plants.

Seasonal Movement

In winter, groups of hunter-gatherers probably congregated on the coast and lived on fish and shellfish. Mounds of discarded shells, called shell middens, are evidence of their presence and have been found along old shorelines on the west coast of Scotland and on some of the islands.

There is also an important local group of middens near the River Forth which began to accumulate shells between 5000 and 4000 BC. The middens are concentrated on the south side of the Forth estuary, at around 15m above today's sea level. Limpets are the main shellfish represented in the west coast middens, while oyster shells dominate in the Forth Valley middens. At Polmonthill, charcoal, burnt stones and hearths were identified within the midden. The midden at Braehead, to the east of Alloa, is one of the few identified on the north side of the estuary and it is the most northerly and westerly of the Forth Valley group of shell middens, dating between 4470-4158 BC.

Braehead Midden

Nearly all of the surviving Scottish shell middens appear to belong to the very late Mesolithic, with some, such as Inveravon, continuing to accumulate after the introduction of cereals and domesticated animals. At Inveravon, Mesolithic dates start around 5000 BC and the midden was still accumulating shells around 2000 BC, which means that people were still gathering seafood even when they lived in more permanent farming communities.

In summer, people may have scattered into small groups and gone to hunt in the hills. The discovery of a possible small summer hunting camp site on Ben Lawers, at 700m above sea level, is particularly exciting as it is unusual for an early inland site to be associated with evidence of occupation. Here a pit containing struck quartz flakes has been dated to 7200-6700 BC. The site has been described as a seasonal hunting stand which was perhaps revisited several times.

Microliths

The most commonly found Mesolithic tools are microliths - from the Greek words meaning 'small' and 'stone'. Examples were found scattered across the site at Ben Lawers along with snapped blades of flint and quartz and quartz knapping debris. Knapping is a technique for working flint and other stone into tools. Microliths are usually identified from the large quantities of waste material produced in their manufacture. They were used in spears and arrows where a number of them would be set into wooden hafts, or handles, using resin, but they were probably also used in food preparation.

Many hunter-gatherer camps would have been of such a temporary nature that firm evidence for their existence may never be found. The presence of a camp might only be recognised by identifying flint scatters or concentrations of shells. Such flint scatters are most often found without context, sometimes during the excavation of later sites e.g. Lower Greenyards, Bannockburn. Some scatters of stone tools confirm that the early Scottish Mesolithic people were part of a wider continental north European tradition.

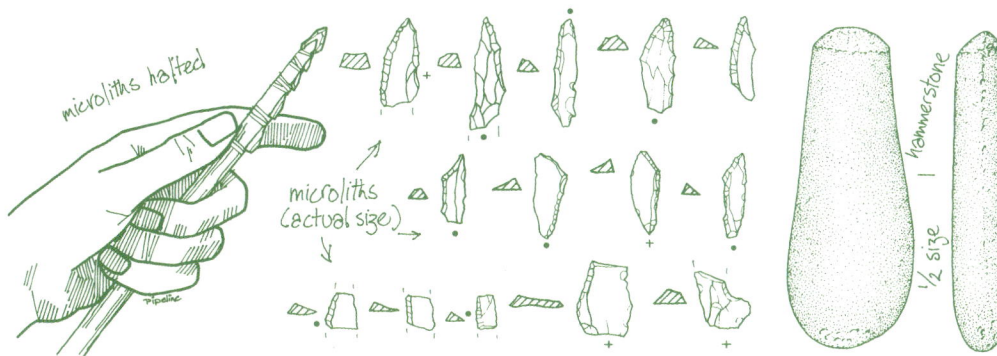

microliths hafted

microliths (actual size)

½ size   hammerstone

Crown Copyright

Other Remains

Most of the early Scottish Mesolithic sites are on the west coast and comprise a few large complex sites. The earliest dated human activity in Scotland, of around 7500 BC, is at Kinloch on Rhum. Here, archaeologists found a wealth of artefacts as well as structures and evidence of hearths. There are also a few early east coast sites, such as the camp site at Fife Ness, near Crail, also dating from around 7500 BC. Here, a possible temporary structure, 2m across, associated with pits with hazelnut shells and worked flint, was situated on the lower part of the late glacial beach. A nearby area of burning may have been a hearth. It is difficult to establish, even at the larger sites, whether they were occupied for long periods of time or for short, regular annual visits. There is currently no evidence to suggest the permanent occupation of any of the camps so far discovered.

No early finds are known from around Stirling, perhaps reflecting the effects of changing sea levels and marine deposition along the banks of the River Forth. In the Stirling area the sea was at its lowest post-glacial level at around 8000-7600 BC. The local environment was rich in natural resources which the hunter-gatherers successfully exploited. The earliest site from the Forth Valley is Pit V at Chapelfield, near Cowie, dated at around 6000 BC. The pit was surrounded by an unusual arrangement of stakes, but its function is unknown. There were no Mesolithic artefacts from Chapelfield.

Pit V at Chapelfield, Cowie
Under excavation
Copyright Glasgow University Archaeological Research Division

Antler mattock from Woodyett, Gargunnock
Copyright Trustees of the National Museums of Scotland

During the nineteenth century a number of whale skeletons were found around Stirling at various depths in the carse clays. These clays were deposited when the tidal estuary of the Forth extended well inland. Between 6000-5000 BC the sea reached as far inland as Aberfoyle. Four of these skeletons were associated with antler tools. One of these tools, the red deer antler mattock found at Woodyett near Gargunnock in 1877 and now in the National Museums of Scotland, has been dated to 4950-4460 BC. It is generally believed that the whales were stranded on the shore, much like the one stranded on the mudflats near Grangemouth in 1997. Hunter-gatherers would not have passed up such opportunities to acquire whale meat and blubber. Some of the whale bones are in the Stirling Smith Art Gallery and Museum.

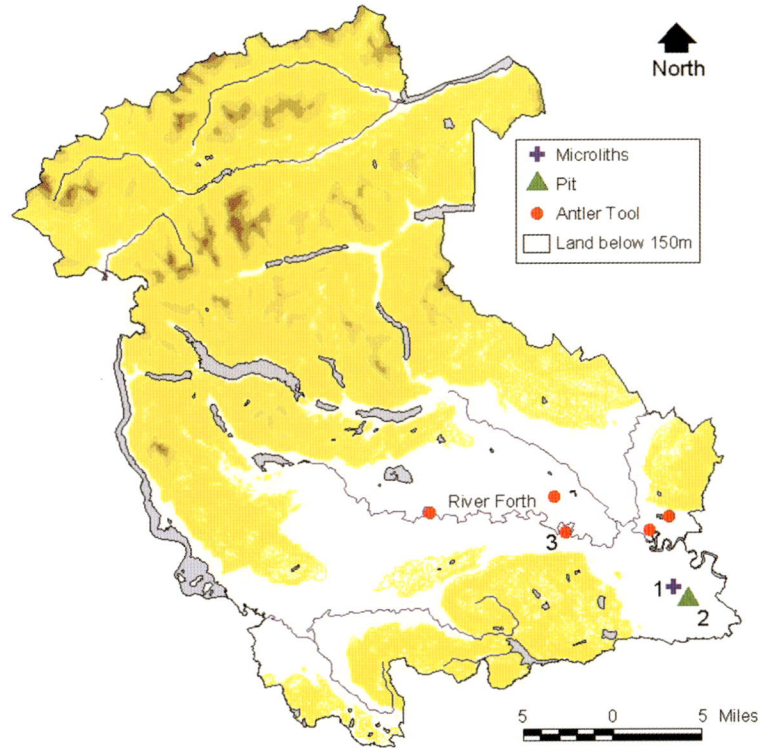

Legend:
- ✚ Microliths
- ▲ Pit
- ● Antler Tool
- ☐ Land below 150m

North

River Forth

1 ✚ ▲
2
3

5 0 5 Miles

Social Organisation

The archaeological record cannot provide direct information on the social organisation of these hunter-gatherers. Anthropological parallels suggest that they were probably grouped into extended family units which periodically met with other similar groups to trade, share resources and forge relationships. Most modern hunter-gathering communities live in broadly egalitarian societies, sharing resources equally among their members. This seems likely to have been the case with our Mesolithic ancestors.

No burials of this period are known from Scotland but there are examples from Scandinavia which show a respect for the dead and bear witness to the existence of family relationships. Finds of perforated cowrie shells recovered from a number of Mesolithic sites probably represent personal adornment, perhaps necklaces, and people may well have made and worn leather clothing similar to that worn by Native North Americans.

Early Farmers
The Neolithic 4000 - 2000 BC
The Evolution of an Agricultural Economy

By around 7500 BC farming had been widely adopted across the Near East, in the areas where cereal crops, and animals such as sheep and cattle, were first domesticated from the wild. By 5000 BC farmers had settled in northern Europe where they grew crops, kept animals, built long timber houses, made pottery, and manufactured polished stone axes.

The Neolithic or New Stone Age began in Scotland around 4000 BC. It is characterised by the use of domesticated animals and cultivated plants which were introduced from continental Europe. However, pollen analysis has identified cereal pollen in Scotland from around 5000-4500 BC, suggesting that farming of some kind was already going on in the period still technically known as the Mesolithic. Some Mesolithic hunting-gathering communities may have readily adopted some of the new ideas being imported into the area by incomers, who brought the domesticated animals, crops and the knowledge to manage them effectively. In other areas the transition from Mesolithic to Neolithic may well have been more gradual.

Saddle Quern
Copyright
Trustees of the National
Museums of Scotland

Neolithic farming required the management of plants and animals to a much greater degree than was necessary in a hunting-gathering economy. The cycle of the seasons was even more important to the success of settled agricultural communities. The early farmers grew wheat, barley, and pulses. In the later Neolithic and into the early Bronze Age barley was the main cereal crop and a few grains were found at the Chapelfield site, near Cowie.

Flour was produced from harvested grain on simple saddle querns, where a small stone was rolled across a flat base stone to grind the grain. Other non-food crops such as flax, which was used for making cloth, were also cultivated. Evidence of actual fields and cultivation systems is rare on mainland Scotland. Narrow ridges for planting crops were probably created using a spade, while hoes and ards (a simple wooden plough) were also used. In some farming communities animal husbandry dominated over arable cultivation, with cattle, sheep, goats and pigs being kept. Some groups may have practised transhumance, where their animals were moved seasonally to fresh upland pastures.

Despite changing practices and improved techniques, the first farmers would still have relied on hunting and gathering. Deer, fish and birds continued to play an important role in their diet along with wild nuts, particularly hazelnuts, and berries. Shell middens continued to accumulate into the Neolithic period. Analysis on material excavated from the midden at Nether Kinneil, which also included pottery and bones of domestic cattle, yielded a series of dates from 3000-2000 BC.

Shell Midden at Nether Kinneil under excavation

The Neolithic also saw the introduction of the technology necessary to make pottery and build large monuments. Neolithic peoples also exploited previously untapped resources, such as stone for the manufacture of polished stone axes.

Impact on the Environment

People had already started to manage their environment in the Mesolithic period, but in a subsistence agricultural economy the primary reason to fell woodland is to clear land for growing crops and to provide pasture. There is clear evidence in the Neolithic period of widespread woodland clearance, perhaps reflecting the continuing mobility, rather than the size, of the population. Wood was used for buildings and fencing with the woodland being managed through techniques such as coppicing, which produces long straight branches. Pollen analysis confirms the decrease of some tree species and an increase in plants reflecting more open conditions and providing evidence for cereal cultivation.

Settlement

On the Scottish mainland the scarcity of Neolithic houses may reflect the difficulty in locating traces of timber structures in the uplands, the damaging effect of later agriculture in the lowlands, and the encroachment of peat in some areas. However, in the uplands stone monuments, especially burial cairns, still survive. In the lowlands, many sites have only been recognised in the last 20 years, identified from the air as cropmarks.

The few examples where evidence does survive in Britain and Ireland suggest that in the early part of the period people lived in small rectangular houses of stone and timber and built their ceremonial structures on a similar plan. The small round stone houses characteristic of the late Neolithic in the Northern Isles, e.g. Skara Brae, are not found on the mainland. It has been suggested that, in some areas, the lack of identifiable Neolithic houses and fields may be because a more nomadic way of life continued from the Mesolithic.

Early/Middle Neolithic artefacts and sites

1. Chapelfield, Cowie
2. Clash Farm, Callander
3. Cowie Road, Bannockburn
4. Parks of Garden
5. Barbush, Dunblane
6. Gillies Hill
7. Sheriffmuir
8. Creag na Caiilich
9. Blair Drummond Moss
10. Cambusmore
11. Ballochraggan
12. Auchenlaich
13. West Bracklinn
14. Severie
15. Uamh Bheag
16. Cromlix
17. Broadgate
18. Glenhead, Doune

Reconstruction drawing of Balbridie Timber Hall
Copyright
David Hogg

Erratum

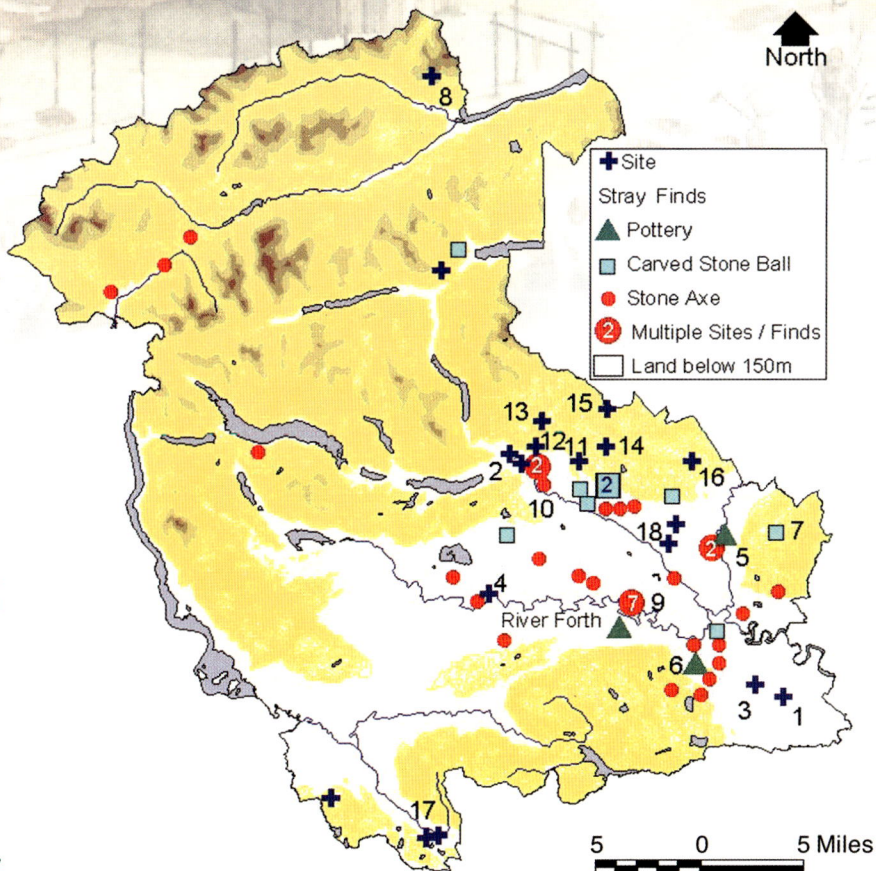

Early/Middle Neolithic artefacts and sites

1. Chapelfield, Cowie
2. Clash Farm, Callander
3. Cowie Road, Bannockburn
4. Parks of Garden
5. Barbush, Dunblane
6. Gillies Hill
7. Sheriffmuir
8. Creag na Caiilich
9. Blair Drummond Moss
10. Cambusmore
11. Ballochraggan
12. Auchenlaich
13. West Bracklinn
14. Severie
15. Uamh Bheag
16. Cromlix
17. Broadgate
18. Glenhead, Doune

North

Site +

Stray Finds

▲ Pottery

◻ Carved Stone Ball

● Stone Axe

② Multiple Sites / Finds

☐ Land below 150m

River Forth

5   0   5 Miles

Only two houses have so far been excavated in Scotland with any real similarity to examples from continental Europe. The timber hall at Balbridie in Aberdeenshire is dated to 3900-3700 BC. The hall measured 24m by 10m and may have been used for communal or ceremonial rather than simply domestic purposes. At Clash, near Callander, a building with a very similar ground plan has been confirmed by excavation (August 2001) to be Neolithic in date. It measured 25m by 9m and was associated with Neolithic pottery. Both sites have been identified from cropmarks.

Plan of structures at Chapelfied, Cowie
Copyright
Glasgow University Archaeological Research Division

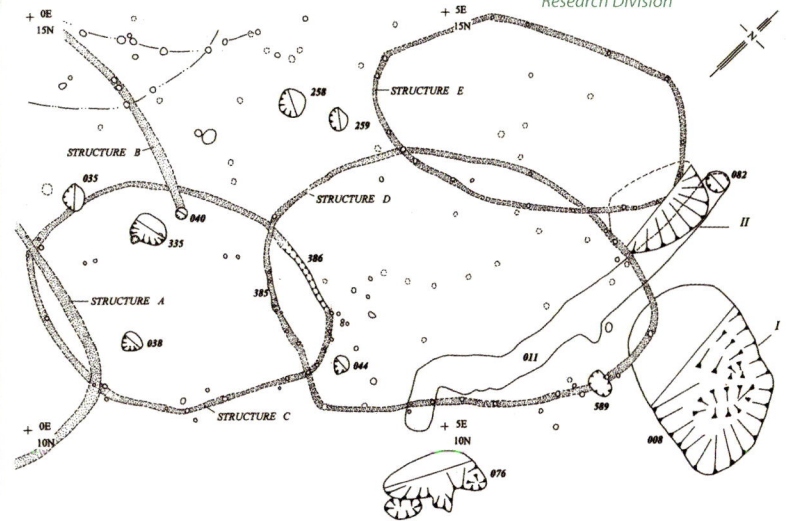

The Neolithic building at the Clash, near Callander, under excavation in August 2001

Chapelfield provides another possible model, but the buildings are not securely dated to the Neolithic period. These structures were oval in shape, constructed of stakes, with no marked entrance and no internal features. One of them, called Structure D, measured 4.4m by 2.8m, and was thought to have been built around 3500 BC.

The building of the oval structures at Chapelfield was associated with the construction of pits. These pits were not for holding upright posts, nor for storage or burial. Instead, artefacts, including early Neolithic pots and fine blades of pitchstone, a stone which comes from Arran and was suitable for flaking into tools, had been deposited in them in a deliberate and structured way. The deliberate and selective deposition of objects in pits is seen elsewhere in Scotland at this date. Chapelfield seems to have been a multi purpose site, serving both a ritual and a domestic use. The former is represented by the pits and the latter by the oval structures. Other stone tools and a saddle quern were also recovered from the site. Evidence from pollen analysis suggests that the area around Cowie in the Neolithic period was a mixed woodland environment.

The pits at Chapelfield were formed into two rows and can be compared to another excavated site at Cowie Road, Bannockburn, only 2km to the west. At Cowie Road there was evidence of a ritual complex comprising two enclosures. One, formed by pits, has been dated between 4034-3816 BC - early Neolithic. The other, made of posts, dates from the middle Neolithic period, 3369-3041 BC. The complex at Cowie Road may be aligned on the site at Chapelfield.

These pit and post enclosures are examples of a type of ceremonial monument known as a cursus, so-called by eighteenth century archaeologists as they resembled a Roman chariot racing track (Latin - cursus). These are ritual monuments and usually comprise long rectangular ditched enclosures, of which there are over 50 known in Scotland.

They are also found in England. However, enclosures defined by parallel lines of pits or posts are a particularly Scottish variation. The cursus at Cowie Road, although incomplete when discovered, was almost 90m long on its southern side.

Another important site lay on the edge of Flanders Moss and showed evidence of Neolithic activity on the floodplain of the River Forth. Excavations at Parks of Garden revealed a wooden platform made mainly of oak timbers and dated to 3340-2920 BC.

No artefacts were found on the platform and this makes its use uncertain. It could have been a platform from which hunting and fishing expeditions were launched across the marshlands or it may have served some unknown ritual function.

Plan of Pit and Post Enclosures at Cowie Road, Bannockburn
(Pit enclosure is shown in blue, post enclosure in red)
Copyright Historic Scotland

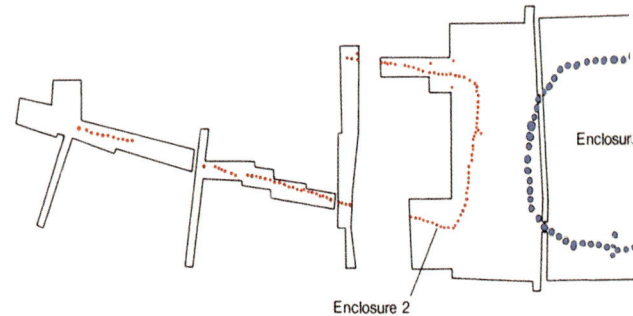

Enclosure 2

0   50 m

Timber Platform at Parks of Garden
under excavation

Reconstructed Neolithic house at Otzidorf, Umhausen, Austria

Artefacts

Neolithic pottery shows variation in both style and decoration. The earliest pots were simple round-bottomed bowls but more elaborate ones were found at Chapelfield and Barbush near Dunblane. Some sherds were also recovered from the later Iron Age fort on Gillies Hill near Stirling. In the late Neolithic a distinctive type of decorated pottery, known as Grooved Ware was produced and was distributed widely in Orkney and in Tayside, Fife and Yorkshire and in the south of England. In the Stirling area only Barbush has produced any of this pottery.

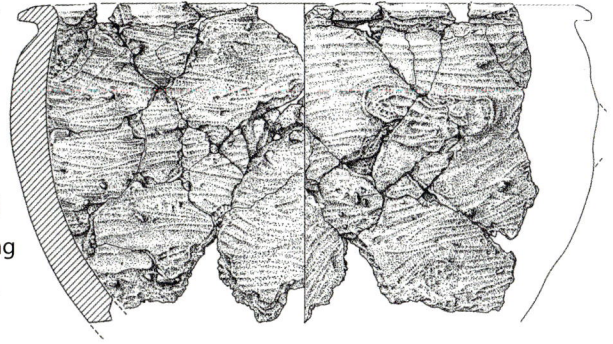

Pottery from Barbush, Dunblane
Copyright Trustees of the National Museums of Scotland

Small blades made from Arran pitchstone, such as those found at Chapelfield, were part of a wider trade in both raw materials and artefacts carried out by early farmers. Around Stirling, evidence of this trade comes mainly from stray finds such as ornamental stone balls

Polished stone axes in the Stirling Smith Art Gallery and Museum
Clockwise from the left –
Braes Farm (Doune),
River Teith,
Blair Drummond Moss, Cambusmore

and stone axes. Nationally, discoveries of ornamental stone balls have been concentrated in Aberdeenshire and north east Scotland. In the Forth Valley, they have been found largely on the Braes of Doune area. The purpose these balls is unknown and may have been ceremonial rather than practical.

Carved Stone Ball from Sheriffmuir, in the Stirling Smith Art Gallery and Museum

Finds of stone axes extend more widely across the Forth Valley than the chambered cairns and stone balls. At Creag na Caillich, near Killin, quarrying of stone for the manufacture of axes was being carried out around 2900 to 2300 BC. Axes of hornfels, the grey-green fine-grained rock from Creag na Caillich, were traded widely across Eastern Scotland and even reached as far away as Buckinghamshire, some 600km to the south. A Killin axe from Blair Drummond Moss is in the collections of the Stirling Smith Art Gallery and Museum. The stone quarry site is on a rock outcrop, 700m above sea level, which seems to have been chosen for its prominence rather than for its ease of access. Further evidence of the spread of these trading links is shown by the analysis of an axe from Cambusmore near Callander, now in the Stirling Smith Art Gallery and Museum, which originated from the Tievebulliagh/Rathlin area in Northern Ireland.

Not all of these polished stone axes were in everyday use; some were too small for practical uses and may have had a more ceremonial function. These show no signs of wear and are often made of special material e.g. jadeite, a material imported into Scotland from either Brittany or the Rhineland. Surviving hafted examples are rare.

Hafted stone axe
Copyright Trustees of the National Museums of Scotland

Neolithic Society and its Monuments

In a more settled community, people establish relationships with the land which are different from hunter-gatherers. They develop different social structures which are reflected in their religious beliefs. People who are organised into larger groups are better able to construct large burial and ceremonial monuments, in both timber and stone. These required co-operation and co-ordination and only became possible with the development of larger and wider tribal groupings.

Chambered Cairn, Edinchip, Lochearnhead

*pyright
toric Scotland*

In the early Neolithic there is no obvious expression of status, either in the goods which people buried with the dead, or in the houses which they built. In some tombs it appears that the bones of the dead had been re-arranged or mixed up after burial and it has been suggested that this may reflect an early Neolithic belief that, after death, people were part of the collective 'ancestors' and not individuals.

Our understanding of Neolithic culture depends on evidence from burial mounds and other ceremonial structures. Nationally, there are more burial monuments recorded than settlements from this period and this is reflected in the Stirling area. Large burial monuments were built from around 4000 BC and probably had a ritual as well as a burial function. Huge communal efforts were required to construct them. Some long mounds were built over timber mortuary structures, while in others stone chambers were built for the deposition of the dead.

In the Forth Valley and much of west and south-west Scotland and the Northern Isles, a range of stone chambers was built. The distinctive chambers of the Forth Valley cairns make them part of the Clyde group of chambered tombs. They are characterised by chambers with overlapping side slabs, and cross slabs which subdivide the chambers. The chambers were then covered by a long mound of stones. Their distribution in this area, concentrated on what is now marginal ground between Callander and Dunblane, suggests a route into the Forth Valley from the south west, with links through the area to Glen Almond, Strathearn and beyond.

Ballochraggan Chambered Cairn
Showing stone chamber

Most of the stone chambers could be re-entered after the original burial for further interments, allowing them to be re-used over a period of time. Almost all excavated cairns have a number of bodies placed together in one tomb. Some of the bodies show evidence that the flesh was removed before burial either through exposure to the elements and wild animals, a process known as excarnation, or by temporary burial elsewhere. None of the Stirling long cairns have been excavated.

The group of tombs on the Braes of Doune shows considerable variety. Stirling can lay claim to Scotland's longest chambered cairn, at 320 metres in length, at Auchenlaich near Callander. It also has at least one unusually high altitude cairn, at West Bracklinn at 328m above sea level - exceptional for a Clyde-type burial. A chamber without a cairn survives at Severie and there is a round cairn with a chamber on Uamh Bheag and one long cairn without field evidence of a chamber at Cromlix. There is also a possible earthen long barrow at Broadgate in Strathblane.

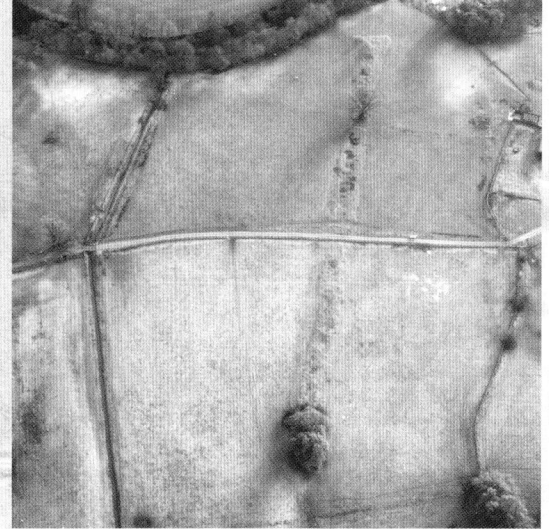

Rectangular ditched enclosures of approximately the same size, shape and date as the long barrows have been recognised in recent years from air photographs, especially in Eastern Scotland. This type of monument is known as a long mortuary enclosure, and was built in the early Neolithic. A very interesting monument at Glenhead, near Doune, has been identified as the remains of either a long barrow or a long mortuary enclosure. Only the side ditches are visible on the aerial photographs. At a similar site at Inchtuthil near Perth, which measured 50m by 10m and was built around 3900 BC, the fenced enclosure was deliberately set on fire.

Possible mortuary enclosure at Glenhead, Doune
(North is at the bottom of the photograph)
Copyright Royal Commission on the Ancient and Historical Monuments of Scotland

Aerial view of Auchenlaich Chambered Cairn
(North is at the bottom of the photograph)
Copyright Royal Commission on the Ancient and Historical Monuments of Scotland

Towards the end of the Neolithic, a number of changes were taking place across Scotland. There is a shift in the archaeological record from burial monuments to ceremonial enclosures. One particularly important type of ceremonial enclosure being built at this time was the henge monument, identified by the presence of a ditch with an external bank and one or two entrances. The intent of this arrangement was not defensive, but it effectively screened the interior from outside view. Excavation inside some henges has confirmed that stone or timber uprights were erected within the enclosed space. There are no henges in the Stirling Council area. However, one of the best known Scottish examples of the henge tradition lies a short distance to the south, at Cairnpapple in West Lothian.

The late Neolithic period was also a time when stones were being erected in circles and rows across Scotland, with local examples at Kinnell (Killin), on Sheriffmuir at Lairhill, and Dumgoyach (Strathblane). Many theories exist about the importance of the alignment of these sites, and it does appear that a number of them relate to major events in the annual movements of the sun and moon. Although stone circles were first built towards the end of the Neolithic, most are thought to belong to the Bronze Age. Excavation has shown that a number were built over pre-existing circles of timber posts. Although the function of the circles can now only be guessed at, they almost certainly included communal activities, both ceremonial and religious. Some were later used as burial sites.

Later Neolithic sites
1. *Kinnell, Killin*
2. *Lairhill, Sheriffmuir*
3. *Dumgoyach, Strathblane*
4. *Nether Glenny*
5. *Gartmore*
6. *Castleton, Cowie*
7. *Duncroisk, Glen Lochay*
8. *Glenhead, Doune*

North

Stone Row at Dumgoyach, Strathblane

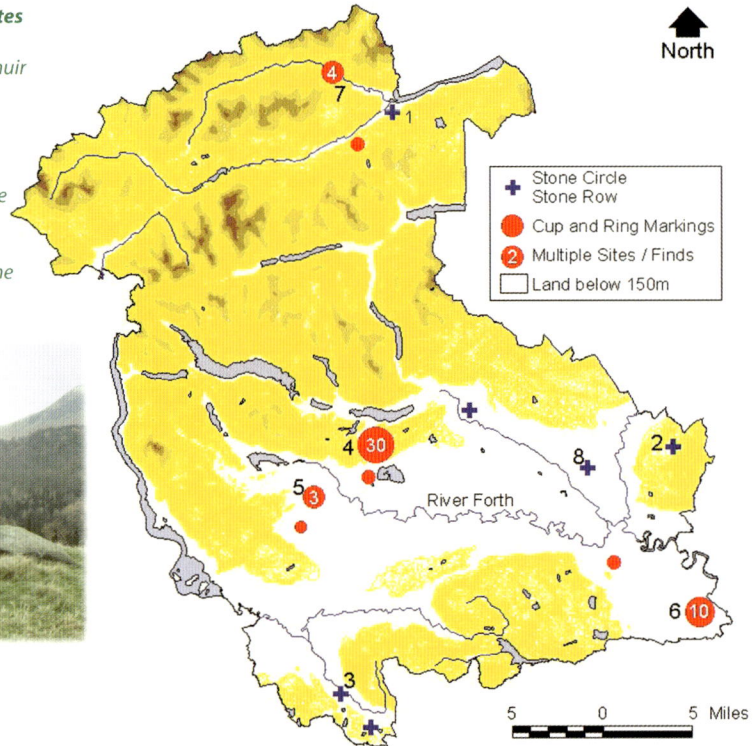

Stone Circle / Stone Row
Cup and Ring Markings
2 Multiple Sites / Finds
Land below 150m

River Forth

5   0   5 Miles

The development of a more hierarchical society towards the end of the Neolithic is reflected in the move towards individual burials in which status in life appears to be reflected in death. The building of chambered tombs ended around 2500 BC.

It is also during this transitional period that the carving of 'cup and ring markings' flourished. These were carved on standing stones and on boulders, but most spectacularly on the living rock. Most are dated to the late Neolithic or Early Bronze Age, although some archaeologists favour an earlier origin, perhaps as early as the fourth millennium. One example was recorded within the long barrow at Dalladies in Angus. Some were incorporated into later monuments e.g. the cist cover slab from Tillicoultry and the slabs re-used in the Iron Age broch at Torwood, near Falkirk. The function of this 'rock art' is not known but it has been suggested that the symbols were route or boundary markers, memorials to the dead, or had an astronomical function associated with the observation and recording of the stars. Perhaps their distribution in some way reflects the practice of transhumance and the location of upland pastures.

Cup and ring marked rock, Gartmore

Rock carvings are often clustered together in particular areas and one such group has been found along the line of the Highland Boundary Fault at Nether Glenny, above Port of Menteith. They have also been recorded at Gartmore in the west, at Castleton near Cowie in the east, and at Duncroisk in Glen Lochay in the north. Some were not designed to be seen, such as the single cup mark on the top of the tall standing stone at Glenhead near Doune.

Cup and ring marked rock at Castleton, Cowie

Early Metal Workers The Bronze Age 2500 - 700 BC
Metalworking - Development, Techniques and Importance

The introduction of metalworking, although revolutionary, was a gradual process and did not involve an invasion of new peoples. A number of changes can, however, be recognised from 2500 BC onwards, although it should be noted that metal tools and weapons were not widely available until the Late Bronze Age. One very significant change is the move from collective to individual burial.

The production of bronze requires two main ingredients - copper and tin. Copper ores are widely available in Scotland and are found locally in the Ochils. However, it is not known if any of these Scottish sources were exploited at this early date. The occurrence of tin is much rarer and it was produced mainly in the south of England and Ireland. Its transport required a network of links which may have already developed with the exchange of earlier stone axes.

Crucible from the Fairy Knowe broch, Buchlyvie
Copyright Trustees of the National Museums of Scotland

Pure copper melts at a temperature of 1083 degrees Celsius. Small bowl furnaces were used in this process. The molten metal which collected in the bowl was then re-melted in a crucible and poured into moulds. Early metalworkers used flat open moulds to manufacture flat bronze axes and the rare stone mould from Glenhead in Carron Valley, now in Falkirk Museum, would have produced just such a tool. Some, like the earlier polished stone axes, were probably used for ceremonial purposes because they were too fragile to use in battle. The smiths who made these objects were highly skilled and must have been important members of society.

Axe mould from Glenhead, Carronbridge
Copyright Trustees of the National Museums of Scotland

The process of metalworking and the distribution of metal products were probably controlled by a small number of people. The spread of metalworking was associated with the increased availability of high quality objects and these in turn enhanced the status of a few individuals. Personal ornaments, such as pins for fastening clothes and bracelets, are commonly found. Fine gold jewellery was worn with either the gold, or, more likely, the finished pieces imported from Ireland. Control over the circulation of these valuable objects enabled these individuals or families to influence the organisation of society. Archaeological evidence suggests there was greater social stratification in the Bronze Age than in earlier periods. Changing beliefs, which manifest themselves in the move to individual burial with grave goods, reflect this changing social organisation.

Settlement and Economy

People grew cereals, both barley and oats, in small fields and kept sheep, cattle, goats and pigs. Some communities may have been more pastoral than arable. Peoples' diet was still supplemented by fish, game and wild plants. The pollen record, however, suggests that there was considerable woodland clearance in the Early Bronze Age, which was associated with the intensification of farming. This seems to have been a period of real agricultural expansion perhaps reflecting the needs of a growing population.

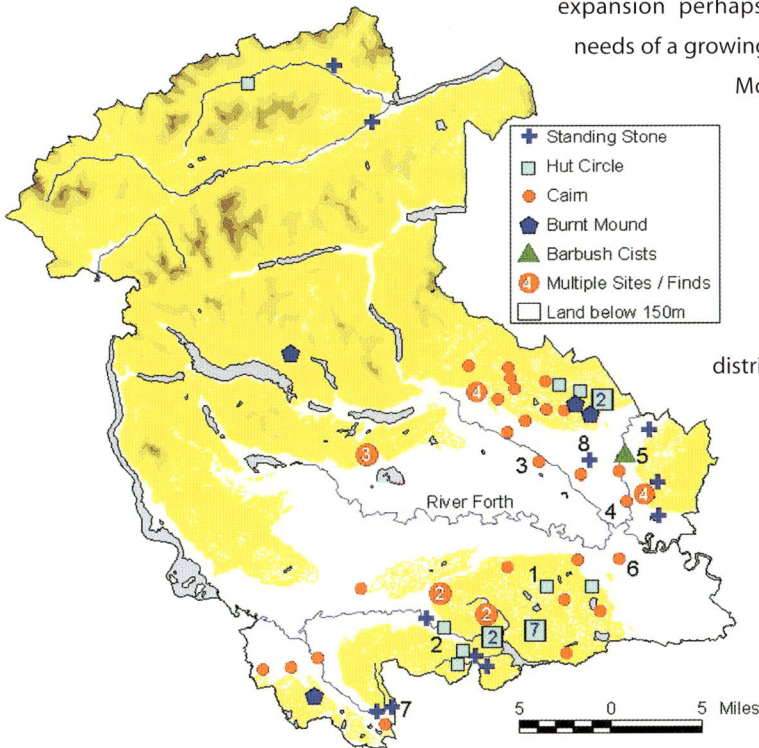

Hut Circle on Touch Muir

More is known about the houses of the Bronze Age than of those belonging to the earlier people. At this time the population reached its widest distribution in prehistoric times, with some upland areas being settled for the first time, perhaps because of increasing population pressure on the lowlands. As these areas have not been subsequently intensively used for agriculture, the remains of early settlements and field systems are still visible above ground in areas now considered as marginal. Many of the hut circles on unimproved pasture and moorland on the Braes of Doune and in Carron Valley belong to the Bronze Age. Although most hut circles are considered to have been built in the Late Bronze Age, a few are dated between 2000-1500 BC e.g. at Lairg in Sutherland.

Legend:
- Standing Stone
- Hut Circle
- Cairn
- Burnt Mound
- Barbush Cists
- Multiple Sites / Finds
- Land below 150m

River Forth

5 0 5 Miles

Bronze Age sites

1. *Touch*
2. *Double Craigs, Fintry*
3. *Deanston*
4. *Fairy Knowe, Bridge of Allan*
5. *Barbush*
6. *Coneypark, Cambusbarron*
7. *Broadgate*
8. *Glenhead, Doune*

The highest recorded hut circle in the Stirling area, at 380m above sea level, is at Double Craigs near Fintry. The term 'hut circle' is given to the field remains of well-built timber roundhouses which are found over most areas of upland Scotland. Although they can occur singly they are often grouped into settlements. All are open and unenclosed. They may be associated with nearby small fields used for growing crops, livestock enclosures, and piles of stones which had been cleared from the fields. Within these open settlements the houses are usually the same size, suggesting that no one family dominated. The surviving low stone/turf walls would have been surmounted by a turf/earth superstructure and roofed in thatch, perhaps of heather or straw. They vary in size, but in the Stirling area most are between 6 and 10m in diameter. Lowland examples do not survive as upstanding features in the modern landscape, having been reduced to cropmarks by ploughing.

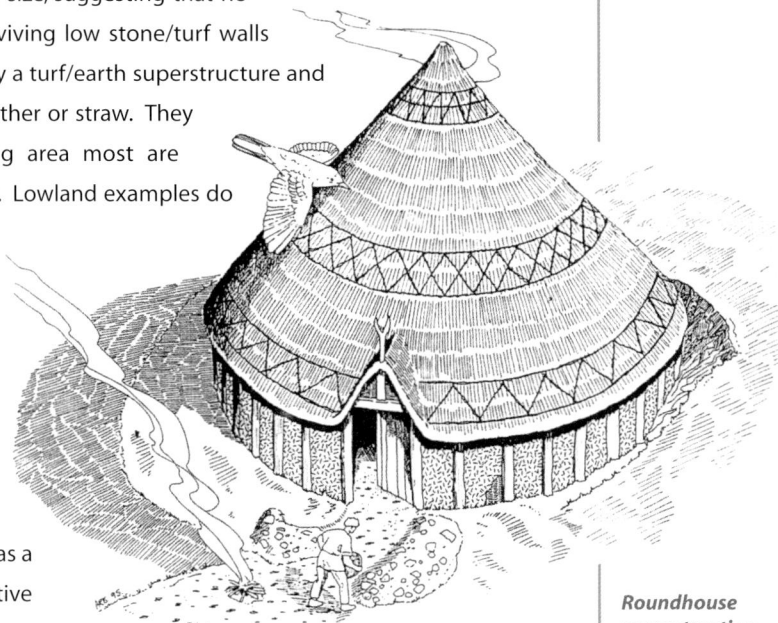

Another type of site belonging to the Late Bronze Age, dating between 1200-700 BC, is known as a burnt mound. These are distinctive horseshoe-shaped piles of stone. Excavation has confirmed that the stones have been either heated or burnt and the mounds often contain evidence of a small tank of stone or timber. Ethnographic parallels with the Native North Americans suggest that these may represent the remains of a communal sauna where stones are heated in a fire and then placed in the tank to create steam. It is also possible that the tanks were used for cooking. A few examples are known from this area - at Strathblane, Glen Finglas and Braes of Doune.

Roundhouse reconstruction
Copyright
Historic Scotland

Burial Practices

However, as there have been few excavations of Bronze Age settlements archaeologists are still highly dependent on information from burial and ritual sites. As with the earlier farmers, more is known about the burial practices of the Early Bronze Age than how people actually lived. In contrast to the multiple burials in the chambered long cairns of the first farmers, the dead were now buried in single graves - a tradition which had already started towards the end of the Neolithic. Both inhumations and cremations are known. The remains were placed in small stone coffins or cists. Inhumations are usually in a flexed position, often accompanied by a pottery vessel or other grave goods such as flint knives, and occasionally more elaborate pieces such as jet necklaces, archery equipment, or bronze daggers.

Food Vessel from Cambusbarron, in the Stirling Smith Art Gallery and Museum

Cremations were often contained within a large pottery urn, known as a Cinerary Urn. The cists were then sealed by a large cover slab and sometimes enclosed in a round mound of earth or stone. Sometimes the covering mounds have been removed by later ploughing.

Excavation has shown that many burials of the period were in simple pits but these are not so easily identified as cist burials. Individual cists may be grouped into clusters and may represent flat cemeteries where the burials were not covered by mounds but must have been marked in some other way, perhaps by the erection of a timber post.

Round Cairn, Deanston

The largest surviving cairn in this area is at Deanston. It is 5m high. Although there is no record of its excavation a central dip in its summit may be a sign of antiquarian activity. Some cairns are found in prominent locations in the landscape and many have outstanding views. No recent cairn excavations have taken place in the Stirling area but excavation on sites elsewhere confirms that not all cairns are simple covering mounds for single cist burials; they can also be very elaborate and complex monuments e.g. North Mains, Perthshire.

Since many cists and cairns were removed by ploughing when archaeological techniques were either not available or not used, an important discovery in this area is the group of three cists at Barbush near Dunblane which was found in January 2000. One cist contained a flexed skeleton and a Food Vessel; another had a disc necklace of cannel coal with a jet fastener, while the third cist was empty. Cannel coal is a type of coal, available locally from the Coal Measures of Central Scotland. Jet is a black stone which takes on a very high polish. The most likely source of the jet is Whitby, in Yorkshire, some 275km to the south of Barbush. The necklace is one of around 30 similar pieces, found mainly in southern Scotland, dating from 2200-1700 BC. Where it has been possible to sex and age the accompanying skeletons they are usually adult females. The Barbush necklace appears to be complete, but has a small overall circumference suggesting that it may have belonged to a child. The skeleton from the second cist is also that of a child, aged 9-12 years, and the accompanying Food Vessel is of a common and widespread type which was current around 2000 BC. The finds from the cists are in Dunblane Museum. There was no evidence that a mound covered any of these cists.

Cist burial with Food Vessel from Barbush, Dunblane
Copyright Headland Archaeology Ltd

Such flat cemeteries were often found in areas of light sand and gravel soils, as at Barbush. Sometimes burials were inserted into natural mounds, as at Coneypark in Cambusbarron. Burials were not always inhumations and cremations were also common. The dead were also placed near monuments which are assumed to be from an earlier period, e.g. the Cinerary Urn containing the cremated remains of a child placed near the standing stone at Broadgate, Strathblane. Different forms of burial may reflect the different roles or status of the individuals buried.

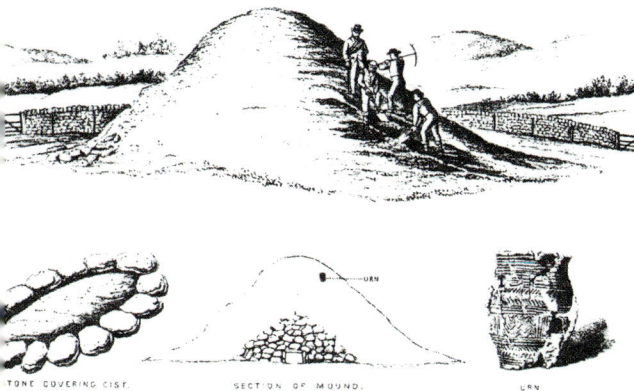

Broadgate
Standing Stone

19th century
excavations of
cairn at the
Fairy Knowe,
Bridge of Allan

Bronze Age pottery shows considerable variety in its form, and Beakers, Food Vessels and Cinerary Urns were the three main types produced. Examples of the different types may be found on the same site, possibly at much the same time, although it is generally accepted that Beaker users were closely involved in the development of early metallurgy in Britain. Pollen analysis suggests that flowers may have accompanied some burials and some of the pots may have contained a mead-like liquid. The increased number of Early Bronze Age burials which have been found, compared to earlier periods, suggests an expansion of the population, perhaps with increased access to the right of burial.

The tradition of raising large stones, which is seen in the earlier circles and rows, continued into the Bronze Age, with both single stones and pairs of stones erected in the Stirling area. Suggestions as to their function are similar to those for the cup and ring markings. In fact a number of the stones have cup marks carved on their surface e.g. at Glenhead near Doune.

Beaker from
Cambusbarron, in
the Stirling Smith
Art Gallery and
Museum

Cannel coal and jet
necklace from cist
at Barbush,
Dunblane
Copyright Trustees of
the National
Museums of Scotland

A Time of Change - the Late Bronze Age

Between 1500 and 600 BC there was a substantial increase in the amount and range of bronze weaponry available, including swords, axes, spears and shields. The famous Blair Drummond wheel, held in the National Museums of Scotland, which dates to 1255-815 BC, is evidence of the availability of wheeled transport in the area at this time. At about the same time, the practice of individual burial in cists or cairns and the construction of large ceremonial monuments, such as stone circles, declined. In the early part of the first millennium BC these changes appear to have been accompanied by a sudden and severe deterioration in the prevailing climatic conditions.

Blair Drummond Wheel

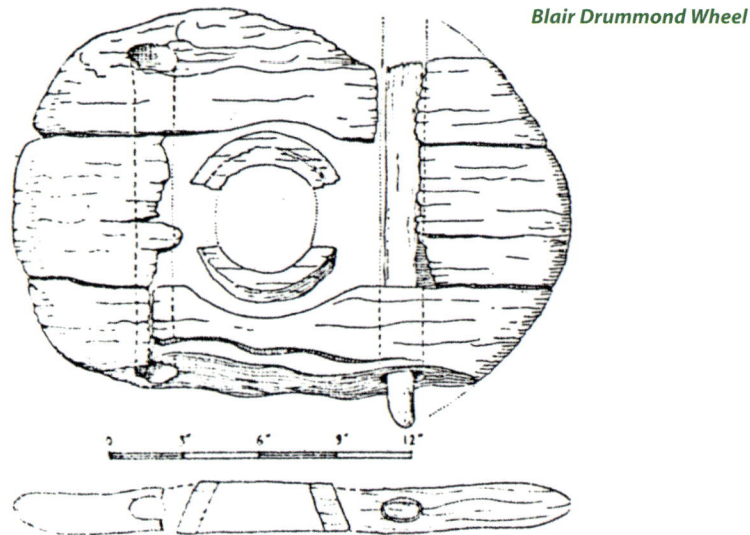

The weather was cooler and wetter and large tracts of densely settled ground, particularly in the Scottish uplands, were lost to agriculture. Heavier rainfall encouraged the growth of peat moorland and the expansion of both upland and lowland peat bogs, which had already begun to develop around 1500 BC, encroached on some areas formerly used for cultivation. All this led to increased pressure on the remaining land and resources, resulting in considerable social upheaval. From around 1000 BC the first houses and settlements defended by a variety of ramparts (banks), walls or palisades (wooden fences) appeared across Scotland, reflecting an increased need for security.

Warriors, Farmers and Artisans
The Iron Age 700 BC – AD 400

The unstable social conditions which had their origins in the Late Bronze Age continued to dominate as the adoption of iron technology was expanding the available range of both tools and weapons. As was seen in the earlier transition from the Neolithic to the Bronze Age, the adoption of this new technology did not involve a wholesale incursion of new people. It seems likely that the power associated with controlling this new technology may have magnified the existing conflict over land and resources which had begun in the Late Bronze Age.

Compasses from the Fairy Knowe broch, Buchlyvie
Copyright Trustees of the National Museums of Scotland

Although iron ore, occurring as bog iron, was more widely available than tin or copper, it is a harder metal than bronze and more difficult to work. Evidence from the broch at Fairy Knowe near Buchlyvie, confirms that the local smiths were able to produce fine, high quality iron products. (All the artefacts from the excavations at Fairy Knowe are in the Stirling Smith Art Gallery and Museum.) Because iron is much harder and longer wearing than bronze, iron swords and spears were more effective in battle than the earlier bronze swords. The introduction of iron tools also made cultivation easier, and farmers could clear larger areas more quickly. The pollen record from a large number of samples from Central and Southern Scotland clearly shows a major clearance episode, from around 500 BC on. While this may have been the result of the need to provide increased areas for both crops and animals, wood and charcoal would also have been required to fuel the hearths, both industrial and domestic, and to satisfy the housing construction needs of a growing population.

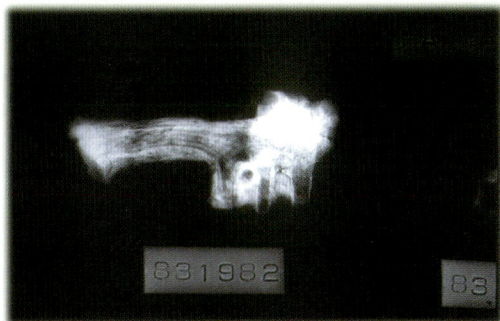

X-ray of Key from the Fairy Knowe broch, Buchlyvie
Copyright Trustees of the National Museums of Scotland

From left to right
Penannular bronze brooches from the broch at Fairy Knowe, Buchlyvie
Copyright Trustees of the National Museums of Scotland

Enamel finger ring from the broch at Fairy Knowe, Buchlyvie
Copyright Trustees of the National Museums of Scotland

Bronze finger ring from Fairy Knowe, Buchlyvie
Copyright Trustees of the National Museums of Scotland

Bronze Armlet from Bows of Doune
Copyright Trustees of the National Museums of Scotland

Bronze continued to be used for luxury objects, especially jewellery such as armlets, brooches, and finger rings. Massive bronze armlets are mainly found in Eastern Scotland and one example, in the National Museums of Scotland, was found locally, at Bows of Doune. It dates from the first or second century AD. All such valuable pieces were made by skilled craftsmen and would have been highly prized. Some items were imported into Scotland from Southern Britain, Ireland and the continent.

Barley was the main cereal crop, although wheat and oats were also grown. In the later part of the Iron Age, rotary querns were used to grind the grain between two circular stones, producing flour for bread, porridge etc. Cattle, sheep, goats, pigs and horses were kept and wild game and plants supplemented the Iron Age diet. People would have worn clothes made of wool, linen and leather.

In contrast to the Neolithic and Bronze Age, no Iron Age burial sites have been found in the Stirling area and they are, in fact, rare in the rest of Scotland. The discovery, near Edinburgh, of a chariot burial, which has been dated to around 250 BC, is therefore exceptional. The chariot, which would have been horse-drawn, was buried intact and this practice shows contact with that part of Europe which is now Belgium and Northern France.

Iron Age pot from Lower Greenyards, Bannockburn
Copyright Historic Scotland

The small quantity of early Iron Age pottery which survives is uniform in style, like the large pot from Lower Greenyards, near Bannockburn, now in the Stirling Smith Art Gallery and Museum. By the late Iron Age native pottery was supplemented by imported Roman wares. It is also likely that the use of wooden and metal vessels was widespread during all prehistoric periods. Wooden objects, in particular, rarely survive. This increases the importance of waterlogged sites such as Oakbank Crannog, on Loch Tay, where well-preserved wooden objects have been found.

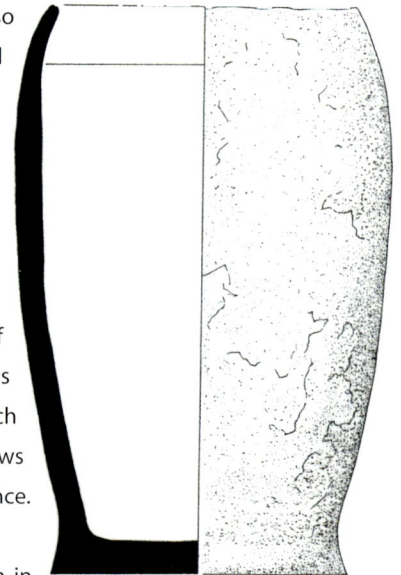

Settlement

Houses and settlements enclosed by wooden palisades were being built from around 1000 BC. They were concentrated in south and east Scotland and many have been identified from aerial photographs. In the Stirling area palisaded homesteads are found in a broad band from Bannockburn and Plean in the east, to Callander in the north and Drymen in the west. The majority of these sites, although enclosed, are not situated in obviously defensive positions. They represent late Bronze Age /early Iron Age farms.

People continued to build this type of settlement for almost a thousand years making precise dating difficult from field remains alone.

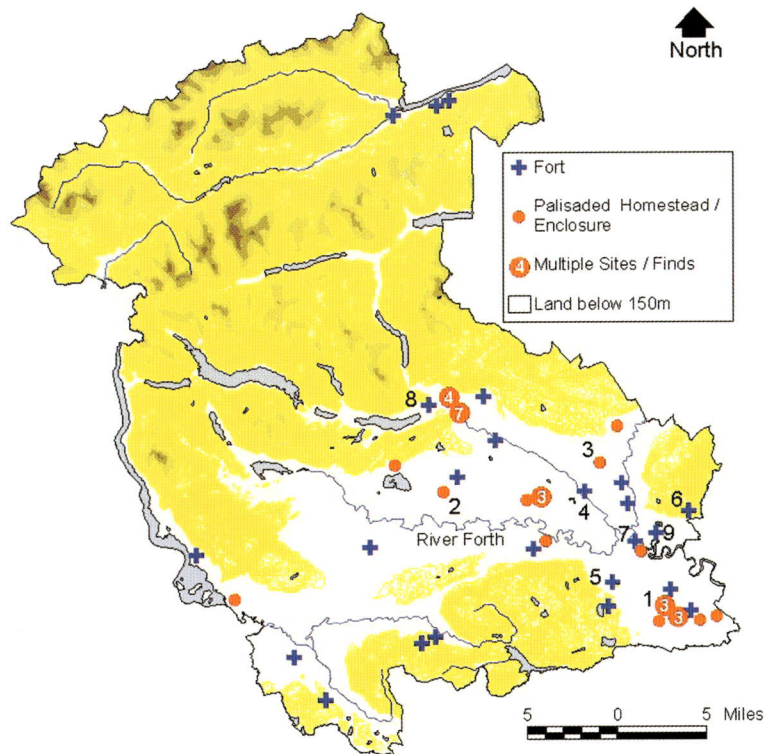

North

Fort
Palisaded Homestead / Enclosure
Multiple Sites / Finds
Land below 150m

River Forth

5   0   5 Miles

Iron Age forts and palisaded sites

1. *Lower Greenyards*
2. *Coldoch*
3. *Easterton*
4. *Easter Row*
5. *Gillies Hill*
6. *Dumyat*
7. *Mote Hill*
8. *Dunmore, Callander*
9. *Abbey Craig*

Oak post in situ at the Roundhouse at Fairy Knowe, Buchlyvie

Below left to right
Coldoch Palisaded Enclosures
Copyright Royal Commission on the Ancient and Historical Monuments of Scotland

Easterton palisaded enclosure
under excavation

Homestead 2 at Lower Greenyards
during excavation Copyright Historic Scotland

Excavated examples show considerable variety in size and plan. In some houses the walls would have been built of wattle and daub, set on a framework of stakes and timber uprights. In other examples, such as Homestead 1 at Lower Greenyards, the walls comprised split timbers set in a continuous circular slot. An additional inner ring of posts was usually erected to support the roof and any upper floors. Local palisaded homesteads generally comprise a single roundhouse of around 15m diameter, built at the centre of an enclosure 40 - 50m wide. A circular house 15m across could have been up to 10m high, easily incorporating an upper storey. It could have accommodated an extended family group of around 20 people.

The house at Coldoch, for example, was 13m in diameter. At Easterton near Dunblane the enclosure measured 46m by 49m and comprised a very substantial palisade trench, up to 0.5m wide and 0.7m deep. Ploughing had destroyed the roundhouse which would have stood at the centre of the enclosure. At Lower Greenyards, Homestead 1 measured 18.6m in diameter within an enclosure about 46m in diameter. On the same site, Homestead 2 had also begun as a house 18m in diameter enclosed by a single palisade. The Homestead 2 house probably belongs to the fifth or sixth century BC.

The defences on some sites became increasingly complex and more substantial, perhaps reflecting increased competition for prestige and power and for control over resources. At Lower Greenyards, Homestead 2, as the house was subsequently enclosed by an increasingly complex set of defensive ditches and palisades it is better described as a fort. Hillforts can be the largest of the enclosed settlements. At Eildon Hill, in the Scottish Borders, some 296 house platforms have been identified. Although not all of these houses would have been occupied at the same time, it is a very substantial settlement.

Reveted outer face of vitrified rampart on the Abbey Craig fort during excavation Copyright Scottish Urban Archaeological Trust Ltd

Some forts may have been permanently occupied, while others may have been used mainly as occasional places of refuge. Forts may also have been communal gathering places, serving a similar function to the earlier ceremonial and monumental henges and stone circles. Excavations indicate that not all hillforts would have been occupied at the same time.

Dumyat Hillfort

Hillforts fall into two main categories - those enclosed by earth ramparts and fronted by ditches, as at Easter Row near Thornhill and Gillies Hill near Stirling, and those surrounded by stone walls, as at Dumyat and Mote Hill, both near Stirling. Included among the stone-walled forts is a group known as vitrified forts. Archaeologists generally only include in this category those forts where burning, either accidental or deliberate, has produced very high temperatures inside the walls, resulting in the fusion of the stone walls with the internal timber lacing - a process known as vitrification. Excavations suggest that many of these date to 700 to 600 BC. The best preserved of the local vitrified forts, at Dunmore near Callander, has five defensive walls. At the Abbey Craig, in Stirling, two phases of defence have been identified on the summit. The earlier wall showed evidence of vitrification. The burnt and reddened revetment walling, which was used to face and contain the rampart core, was clearly visible in the excavation trenches.

Brochs, Duns and Crannogs

By the first century BC the evolution of the roundhouse tradition had resulted in the development of three particular types of smaller defended sites, all of which are found in this area - brochs, duns and crannogs.

Brochs are found mainly in north and west Scotland. However, there is a group of brochs in the Forth Valley which all lie close to areas of good arable land along the fringes of the River Forth. Brochs in lowland Scotland should be seen as a very specialised development of the traditional roundhouse. They were clearly built to impress and many of them are located on prominent sites. Their construction reflects the exceptionally high status of their occupants, which is confirmed by the high quality objects found during archaeological excavations at two local sites, Fairy Knowe at Buchlyvie and nearby Leckie.

Excavation of the broch at Fairy Knowe revealed that it was built and occupied during the first century AD, i.e. the period of Roman involvement in Central Scotland. At Fairy Knowe the broch is circular in plan, with a narrow entrance passage leading through the walls which were 5.4m thick. The entrance faced east towards the rising sun. Stairs within the walls would have given access to the upper floors. It had a central hearth for heating and cooking and there was evidence of the sub-division of the interior space. Some areas may have been used for sleeping while others were used for food preparation. The broch was probably roofed in thatch.

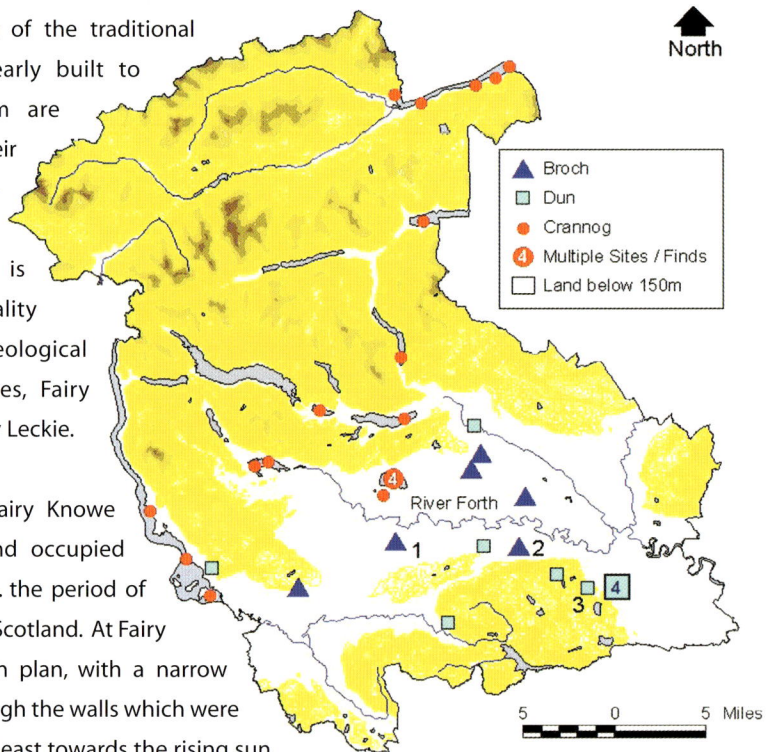

North

Legend:
- ▲ Broch
- ▢ Dun
- ● Crannog
- ④ Multiple Sites / Finds
- ▢ Land below 150m

River Forth

5   0   5 Miles

As well as evidence of contact with the Roman forces the finds from the broch confirmed that its occupants were engaged in leather and woodworking as well as metalworking. Analysis of both iron and copper-alloy artefacts confirmed that their smiths were re-melting Roman metal to fashion tools and ornaments to their own specifications.

Duns are another form of substantial stone-built house whose main area of distribution is Argyll, Galloway and Central Scotland. Duns were often built on hilltops with strategic outlooks. They are generally less complex than the brochs and there is little evidence that they were more than a single storey in height. They can either take the form of a single house or enclose a small group of houses. There is a group of duns in the valley of the upper Bannockburn. At Castlehill Wood the discovery of Roman glass confirms that this group was probably occupied at roughly the same time as the local brochs.

A third type of roundhouse which was being constructed at this time is called a crannog. An artificial, or partly artificial, island, built in water or boggy areas out of boulders and timber piles, provided a solid platform for a timber roundhouse. The crannog was often linked to the shore by a walkway. Most crannogs are now submerged. They are found in many upland lochs, with particularly important groups in Loch Lomond, Loch Tay and Lake of Menteith.

Excavations at Oakbank crannog, on Loch Tay, have been very productive because of the preservation of organic materials in the waterlogged environment. Radiocarbon dates suggest that crannogs were first built around 500 BC, but they continued to be built and used as a house type until later historical times. Some were occupied at the time of the Roman invasion of Scotland, implying an overlap with some of the brochs and duns.

In the absence of archaeological excavation the relationships, if any, between palisaded homesteads, hillforts, brochs, duns and crannogs and their occupants remain unclear.

From top
Interior of the broch at the Fairy Knowe, Buchlyvie

Castlehill Wood dun

Reconstructed Crannog at Kenmore on Loch Tay

Romans and Natives AD 79 – 400
Invasion AD 79 – 83

The Romans had been established in Southern Britain since AD 43. A new governor, Julius Agricola, had arrived in Britain in AD 77. When the Emperor Vespasian died in AD 79, his son Titus re-appointed Agricola with orders to consolidate Roman holdings as far north as the Forth. The skills of the Roman Legions as engineers, as well as being a formidable fighting force, undoubtedly assisted in their rapid and effective occupation of Southern Scotland by AD 80. When Domitian succeeded Titus in AD 81 the army pushed further northwards.

In the Stirling area, the Romans would have found a well-established and successful mixed farming community, divided into a number of tribal chiefdoms, led perhaps by the wealthy families who built and occupied substantial roundhouses, such as the brochs at Fairy Knowe and Leckie. These families had links to Iron Age communities elsewhere in Scotland and had trading contacts across the North Sea. The main tribe identified by the Romans in Central Scotland is the Damnonii, but the precise boundaries of their territory are not known. The confederacy of tribes from the areas north of the Forth, who came together to resist the Roman invaders but were defeated by the Roman army at the battle of Mons Graupius in AD 83, were described collectively by the Romans as the Caledonians.

Roman Legions on the March

At the end of each day's march Roman soldiers established a defended camp. They dug a V-shaped ditch, throwing the excavated material up to form an inner rampart and setting up wooden stakes on the bank. They pitched their leather tents in rows inside these defences. A camp of 25 hectares could house up to 20,000 men, the equivalent of two legions with supporting staff. One of 16 hectares could support around 11,000 men, representing one legion and full support.

Antonine Wall, Croy Hill, sculpture of three legionary soldiers
Copyright Trustees of the National Museums of Scotland

A few camps survive as earthworks, including a small part of the camp at Malling near Port of Menteith. Most, however, have been identified from aerial photographs as cropmarks. These show the ditches which were dug and the extra defences which were built to defend the vulnerable gateways into the camps. The majority of camps were built to the traditional playing card design, with straight sides and rounded corners. It may even be possible to identify particular groups of camps with particular campaigns by studying their shape, size, the design of the gateways, and their relationship to other Roman features. For example, those associated with the first century campaigns of Agricola have a tendency to be square, and often have complex entrance defences, known as Stracathro gates, which are known only from Scotland. All camps with this type of gate lie in areas associated with Agricola's campaigns.

Local examples are found at Malling at Port of Menteith (5 hectares) and Bochastle near Callander (19.4 hectares). It may even be possible to identify particular legions from the designs used in the camp construction. Those with Stracathro entrances are thought to be the work of the Second Legion Adiutrix, based at Chester.

At both Malling and Bochastle the camps probably housed the men involved in building the adjacent forts.

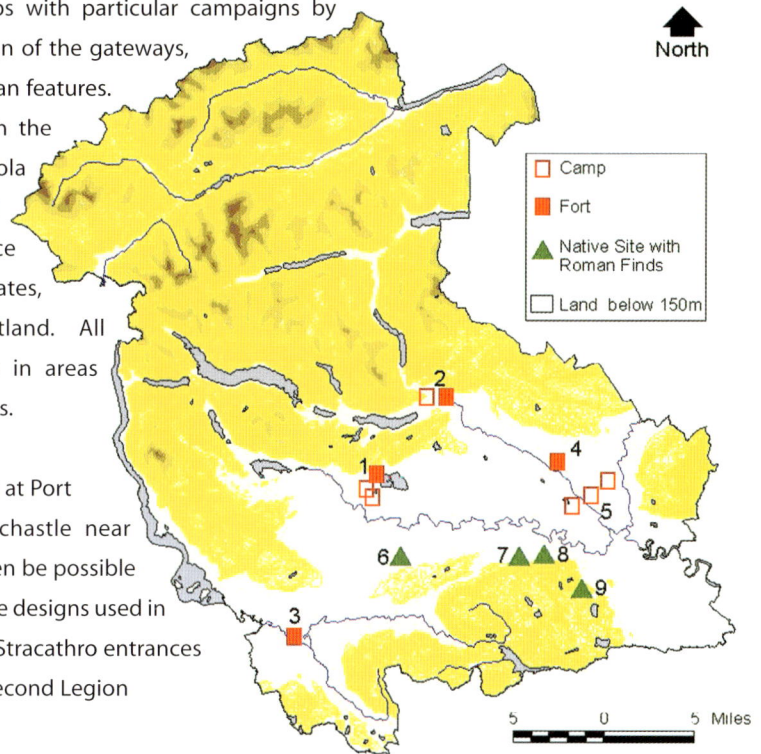

Roman forts and camps

1. Malling,
   Port of Menteith
2. Bochastle,
   Callander
3. Drumquhassle,
   Drymen
4. Doune
5. Craigarnhall
6. Fairy Knowe,
   Buchlyvie
7. Leckie
8. Keir Hill,
   Gargunnock
9. Castlehill Wood

North

☐ Camp
■ Fort
▲ Native Site with Roman Finds
☐ Land below 150m

5   0   5   Miles

The Frontier Occupation

The first century or Flavian frontier (named after the Emperor Vespasian's family) comprised a chain of forts linked by a network of roads and signal stations. This frontier included forts at Drumquhassle near Drymen, Malling, Bochastle and Doune. They were built after the battle of Mons Graupius in AD 83. Only the fort at Bochastle still has its western ramparts visible as earthworks. The others have been identified from air photographs as cropmarks. These forts controlled access to and from the main highland glens to the north.

Doune Roman fort building foundations under excavation

The forts at Malling, Bochastle and Doune all have distinctive entrances known as 'parrot's beak'. This is where the ditches on both sides of the entrance meet and curve inwards towards the entrance. Such a defensive form was not used after the Flavian period. The distribution of forts with these entrances follows closely that of camps with Stracathro-type gates. They may also be the work of the Second Legion Adiutrix. The forts were probably built by legionary troops but would have been garrisoned by auxiliary troops. There is currently no information available on the units which garrisoned these forts.

Doune Roman Fort Base of bread oven under excavation

During excavations within the fort at Doune, a number of foundation trenches were identified which formed two wings of a building arranged either side of a central corridor. One possible interpretation is that it served as the fort's hospital. A row of five circular stone-based bread ovens was found just inside the western rampart of the fort as well as traces of one of the internal roads.

Bochastle Roman fort Copyright Royal Commission on the Ancient and Historical Monuments of Scotland

Contact with the Local Population

Excavations at four native sites in the Forth Valley, namely the brochs at Fairy Knowe and Leckie, the palisaded homestead at Keir Hill, Gargunnock and the dun at Castlehill Wood, have revealed evidence of contact with the Roman forces occupying the area during the first century AD. It is important to note that all four sites lie behind the Roman front lines in this area confirming a friendly relationship with the local tribes. The artefacts from the broch at Fairy Knowe provide a valuable insight not only into the culture and economy of the broch's occupants but also into their relationship with the Roman army.

Roman glass and pottery from the broch at Fairy Knowe Buchlyvie
Copyright Trustees of the National Museums of Scotland

As of Vespasian AD 69-79 from the broch at Fairy Knowe, Buchlyvie
Copyright Trustees of the National Museums of Scotland

Roman pottery, glass and coins from Fairy Knowe are all of late first century AD date. The native population most readily acquired Roman material such as this while the Roman army was in the local area. The closest Roman fort to Fairy Knowe is at Malling, only some six kilometres to the north, across the River Forth. The range and quality of the Roman goods from the broch, especially the Samian, a fine reddish coloured pottery initially made in Gaul, confirms its high status and important contact with the Roman army. Indeed the variety of Samian forms present on the site puts it on an equal footing with sites in England which subsequently developed into villas. Since no second century Roman artefacts were found at the broch its occupation had ended before the building of the Antonine Wall.

The Withdrawal

The Roman army was withdrawn from the areas north of the Forth in AD 86/7, after only a few years of occupation. It returned to Central Scotland in the second century and built the Antonine Wall in AD 142/3 as a permanent physical barrier across Central Scotland between the estuaries of the Forth and the Clyde. As much of the Stirling area lay to the north of the Antonine Wall there is little evidence of Roman activity here in the second century. However, the Roman road north through the Antonine Wall to the fort at Ardoch, near Braco, and beyond, passed through what is now the King's Park area of Stirling, and may have crossed the Forth upstream of the town. A fort, whose location is not known, may have guarded this crossing point.

The Antonine Wall was abandoned in the AD 160s and the army retreated south to Hadrian's Wall. However, the northern tribes were constantly threatening to over-run this frontier. The Roman response was a series of Imperial expeditions aimed at quelling once and for all these disturbances north of the Wall. The Emperor Septimius Severus himself led the campaign, between AD 208-211. The temporary camp at Craigarnhall, south east of Doune is the only site in the Stirling area thought to date to this period. Here a large 25-hectare camp is thought to belong to the Severan campaigns.

Roman involvement in Central Scotland ended with the death of Severus. The native peoples who had continued to live and farm in the area around Stirling during the Roman occupation still remained after the departure of the Roman army. Here they awaited the arrival of Christianity, the emergence of Pictland and the eventual creation of the Scottish Nation. However, that, as they say, is another story.

Acknowledgements

I am grateful to friends, colleagues and my husband who commented on drafts of this book. However, any errors or omissions are the sole responsibility of the author. The assistance of Stirling Council staff, in both the Communications Unit and in the Technical Support Team of Environmental Services, is also appreciated. Thanks are also due to the following organisations and individuals for their permission to reproduce their copyright illustrations: Historic Scotland, The Royal Commission on the Ancient and Historical Monuments of Scotland, The Trustees of the National Museums of Scotland, Headland Archaeology Ltd, Glasgow University Archaeological Research Division, The Scottish Urban Archaeological Trust Ltd, Jim Rideout, and David Hogg.

The Author

Lorna Main has been a local authority archaeologist for many years and is now Stirling Council's Archaeology Officer. She is a Fellow of the Society of Antiquaries of Scotland, on whose Council she currently serves, and is a former Secretary and Chair of the Association of Regional and Island Archaeologists.

Copyright © Stirling Council 2001

Further Reading and Sources of Additional Information

Further Reading

Wild Harvesters, Bill Finlayson, Canongate 1998
Scotland's First Settlers, Caroline Wickham-Jones, Batsford 1994

Farmers, Temples and Tombs, Gordon Barclay, Canongate 1998
Neolithic and Bronze Age Scotland, PJ Ashmore, Batsford 1996

Settlement and Sacrifice, Richard Hingley, Canongate 1998

A Gathering of Eagles, Gordon Maxwell, Canongate 1998
Roman Scotland, David Breeze, Batsford 1996

Additional Sources of Information

This book is based on information on individual sites and objects which is held in the Stirling Sites and Monuments Record. The Record includes copies of old maps, photographs, published excavation reports etc. It is available for public consultation during office hours in the Stirling Council Offices, Viewforth, Stirling by prior appointment with the archaeology officer who can be contacted on 01786 442752. A number of the sites which are illustrated have been discovered as a result of fieldwork, including excavation, which has been undertaken as a requirement of Stirling Council in their role as the planning authority for the area.

Printed by J. Thomson Colour Printers Ltd, Glasgow.